CECELIA

Cause of

Death

My Mother's Story

A Memoir

Angie K. Olson

Copyright

ISBN: 9781794386815

Dedication:

To all my siblings and

to my very patient husband.

TABLE OF CONTENTS

When I was barely ten years old, my mother died in a house fire at our home farm. The coroner stamped her official *cause of death,* _____. When anyone would ask me how my mother died, I would just say, " she died in a farm accident." And then, I would move away or change the subject, hoping they wouldn't ask any more questions. She died a very long time ago; it was in late February of nineteen fifty-one. And yet, throughout the years, whenever my siblings would get together, somehow the conversation would most often drift towards our mother. What really happened that day in February? It has haunted Cecelia's children but also the neighbors that lived nearby, and now, grandchildren who want to know about their grandmother. What happened to her? What was she like? Why did she die so young?

This is my attempt to pass along Cecelia's legacy, as well as maybe find more closure to her life and death. With every word that I captured, I am truly amazed at how much I have remembered from those years long past.

Chapter 1

Cecelia was born in June of 1911, the same year of the horrific Triangle Shirtwaist Company fire in New York. That disaster, killed over one hundred and twenty young women, who were desperate to escape the inferno; and to their demise, found only locked doors.

My mother was the only daughter of a struggling dirt farmer in north central Minnesota. Her mother died when she was not yet of school age, and I can just imagine, it was difficult for her dad, to raise a child by himself. It was the height of the depression, with long food lines in Americas big cities, and for many, nowhere warm to sleep. I expect Cecelia's father was not much better off, as farms in this part of Minnesota struggled to raise enough animals for meat, and to grow enough vegetables to sustain themselves. I wouldn't be surprised if he was anxious to marry

Cecelia off to a local boy, or for that matter, any man that would ease the burden of a mouth to feed. I also suspect her father was in ill health at the time.

**

Cecelia was a lovely young girl, with wavy brown hair and sparkling hazel eyes. She never failed to turn a head or catch a glance from the wondering eye of a man. It wasn't long before she was saying "I do," to Joe W., a boy of almost twice her age. Joe W. was a son of a German immigrant, who came to America in the late 1800s. Joe stood at least six foot three, sandy-blonde hair and blue eyes – and had a commanding presence about him. Joe's father was born in the south-west part of Germany, the same area where Hitler's loyalist lived and trained. It was July of 1928, when Cecelia and Joe W. were married in a Catholic church, close to Camp Ripley near Little Falls. They moved to a farm in the area to start their life together. With only a few years of schooling, 3rd grade education, Cecelia must have felt fortunate to marry such a handsome, and well-established man with land of his own. I would expect, the land was originally homesteaded by his father.

Cecelia had just turned seventeen.

***

While the flappers were kicking up heals in Chicago and mobsters were executing other mobsters on those same streets and in dark alleys, Cecelia was pregnant with her first child.

The stock market crashed in 1929, shortly after their first child was born. A year later, another child and another, and then twins (boy and girl) in 1935. First it was the depression, and then the dust bowl hit hard, ending any chance of eking out a living on this small fruitless farm. Top soil was twirling in the air and landing in other states or in Canada, leaving what little surface soil left full of rocks and debris. That was the last of the dirt farmer. Joe W. lost what little he had as a farm, and headed for California with promises to make his so-called fortune, and send money back to Minnesota for Cecelia and for their five children. The months passed, and no Joe, and no money came to care for the children. She was on her own..

Chapter 2

Penniless and homeless, Cecelia and her children were cut adrift to fend for themselves in a world she knew nothing about, except for a few miles in either direction. I understand her father had already died, and she had no other relatives that could help her with a place to live. She turned to her husbands' family, Joe W's sister and husband, and they took her in. They were also poor farmers. A few weeks went by, and I imagine the strain on everyone was showing. Cecelia had no other choice, but to find a home for her family, and also some means of support. It was nearing fall, and the weather would be changing soon, and it would only delay finding a place to live with so many small children. The twin babies were born the previous June, and were only a few months old.

Cecelia was just a mere twenty-four years old, when she answered an ad in a farmer's magazine, for a housekeeper, for a father and son who owned a farm in south-central Minnesota. The farmer also said that they would take in all her children. It didn't take her long to accept the offer. I doubt if the proposal included any pay, but she was desperate to find a home for herself and her children.

As it turned out, not all the children went with Cecelia. Joe's sister was very fond of the 3rd child, and asked if #3 could live with her, and they would raise her and send her to school. So that is the way it went - Cecelia and four of her children, # 1, 2, 4 and 5 moved to a farm south of Hutchinson, MN, with the two bachelors. The elder (Joe) was in his seventies and the son, known as FJ, was in his mid-forties. FJ was about six-foot-tall, fair complexion with sandy-blonde hair, clear blue eyes and that handsome looking chiseled face, so common with the Germans. FJ's father had also immigrated in the late 1800s from the same part of Germany as Cecelia's first husband's father.

I suppose FJ eyed the children over, wondering how soon they would be old enough for farm work. I imagine this was somewhat like the orphan trains that brought children from cities out east like New York. During the depression years, the trains would head west towards the farm country, and stop at the small towns where bidders would pay for the children based on their physical appearance, usually strength. The children were accompanied by an adult on the train-trip, usually a woman, who made sure the children all looked their best while standing on the train platform, waiting to be looked over by potential bidders. These were hardship years, that forced parents without income, to relinquish their children to hopefully a better life; at the least, enough food and a roof over their heads. And, if they were lucky, they would even be sent to school.

FJ picked up Cecelia and the children in his Model-A-Ford, and loaded up their few personal belongings and headed south to his farm. Cecelia had the twin babies bundled up and balancing on her lap, as a cloud of dust followed the black Ford as it bumped along dirt and gravel roads. After a few hours, the road curved around Whitney Lake, and within minutes the farm was in sight.

***

Cecelia was not at all surprised by the meager farmhouse; a rather colorless,, white-washed, two story clap-board, with blue smoke twirling from the chimney. The Ford headed down the dirt driveway, and rattled and bounced across a wooden bridge, with a meandering stream below. The creek slowly rippled over rocks, as it curved through the pasture, and and skirted the red barn by the house. Hanging low over the water were an abundance of huge Cottonwood trees and sprawling Willows. I imagine Cecelia thought that the creek was nice.

The house was most likely very similar to the modest farm house where she grew up; simple, straight lines that were the easiest to construct by the settlers. Most immigrant farmers came with some practical skills, so that they could build their own houses and other farm buildings. It was common for neighbors to

help each other, and if they hadn't experience in building a structure, they could usually figure it out. They were the typical structures of the time.

There was only a cold-water pump mounted next to the kitchen sink. The wood-fired cast-iron cookstove was used for partial heating of the house as well as all the stove-top cooking and oven baking. There was a living room/sitting room, kitchen and pantry on the main floor and a cold porch/vestibule at the house entrance. Coats and boots were left here as they most often reeked of manure.. A kerosene stove, in the living- room, warmed the main part of the house, and gravity took heat up through an open register in the ceiling. That was the only heat-source to send heat to the upper bedroom. From the kitchen, a narrow steep stairway, snuck around the chimney to an open room at the top of the stairs. Upstairs, there was a bedroom off to the left, and a room over the kitchen, with two or three beds that later would be called the men's room. The cellar was accessed through the pantry floor, that was right off the kitchen.

Outside, towards the creek was an outdoor privy with the Sears Catalog for toilet paper.

***

Somehow, everyone fit in this modest farm house, and it was the start of a new life for Cecelia and four of her children.

The upstairs bedroom with the heat register, became Cecelia's room with her children. She brought a crib along for the babies, and there were two double beds, one for the two girls, # 1 and # 2, and a bed for herself. The room had a small closet to hang clothes, and another closet with shelves. At first, she didn't have a dresser with drawers, but she made due. The room had two windows looking south that somewhat warmed the room when the sun was shining. It also was the brightest room in the house.

Chapter 3

It wasn't long before Cecelia began scrubbing floors and walls and preparing meals for her new family. Her spirited energy gave a new life to the bland air that hovered over the bachelors. She was cheerful and very-well organized and insistent on order in the house. Everything has its place, and that is where you put it. Coats were hung up, shoes by your bed (unless they were boots, they were left by the front door) and nothing was left on the floor. I remember her saying, "If it is on the floor it will be considered trash, and will be thrown away." I don't think she ever threw anything away, but nobody took any chances. Whenever we were asked to do anything, it came with, "if you do this, you can do that," and then a little hug or a peck on the cheek. It all seemed fair.

***

Her first winter on the farm, came and went quickly, and by spring the twins were walking and Cecelia was ready to tackle what needed to be done outside the house. A very small lawn around the house had been kept cut with a manual lawn-mower. If you pushed the mower, the blade twirled and cut the grass. The lawn kept getting bigger and bigger, as Cecelia kept pulling weeds and using a scythe. (FJ sometimes helped, when the weeds were too big and too tall.) She kept pushing the mower in a wider circle, and it wasn't long before the yard was a good size for the children to play. The yard came to life with colorful Peonies, Old Fashion Rose Bushes and Bridal Veil planted on the perimeter. Once old enough, the children all shared the pushing of the lawn-mower and weeding the flower-beds. "One more round and you can have a glass of cool-aid." "One more round and fresh peanut-butter cookies will be waiting," Cecelia would say.

When I was about two years old, Cecelia and I planted a spruce tree that was the same height as I was at the time. She said it was my tree, and I had to make sure it was watered to make it grow. I remember measuring myself against the tree, and, for the first few years, we were even. Then the tree had a bigger burst of growth than me, and there was no catching up.

There was also an apple tree not too far from the house, that as the children grew, became a great tree to climb, especially when the apples were ripe. Cecelia would say, " Pick one to eat, and enough for a pie, but don't pull the apples off the branch, only twist them off, or you damage the branch and it won't have an apple for a few years." When I was older, I loved being up in that tree late in the day as the sun was setting. I felt like I was hiding, and maybe I was. It was so peaceful and quiet, and I was also usually too high for the mosquitoes to nip at my arms and legs.

We also had a plum tree, but we were lucky if the tree produced many edible plums as it would be late in the fall before they would ripen. Often the frost would come first and ruin the fruit. Whatever plums that were salvaged were most likely canned in the fall with the rest of the fruit.

Chapter 4

Just after the Hindenburg exploded over Staten Island, Cecelia gave birth to a girl, # 6, in May of 1937. On November 1, of that year, she and FJ were married in St. Cloud. It was not easy to arrange their marriage as both were Catholic, and the church did not acknowledge divorce, much less a birth before marriage. So, they were married in a civil ceremony. Cecelia continued to attend the local Catholic Church close to the farm, going to Saturday confession and Sunday Mass, and I believe so did FJ. However, she was not permitted to take communion, and yet she did everything else at the church. She helped with meals for weddings and funerals, and everything else Christian Mothers did for people in need. She now shared a bed with FJ. The main floor sitting room was made into a bedroom, with a curtain on a rod to private the room from the living-room.

***

In July of 1939, the year the World's Fair was off and running in New York, Cecelia gave birth to a boy, # 7. The threat of the US heading to war was on the minds of everyone. People had to conserve on gasoline, and started to stock up on food that would soon be rationed, and maybe not available at all in the near future. FJ's thinking was no different. In the cellar, behind the steep steps and out of sight, were bags of sugar, cans of coffee and even wads of FJ's chewing tobacco.

In December of 1940, as France fell to the Germans and Europe is begging America for help in the war, child #8 (girl) is born to Cecelia. By now, #1 is almost twelve years old. The house was full with seven children and three adults.

6, #7, #8

It is 1941, and the Japanese launched an attack on Pearl Harbor and America was officially at war in the Pacific. Most of American's factories were turned into war machines, building tanks, jeeps and whatever the US military needed to fight the battles in the Pacific. The US was already sending war equipment to Europe, but soldiers were not committed to the war effort on the European front at that time. Auto production virtually stopped along with most equipment for domestic use.

Somehow, the farm life was somewhat isolated from the war except for the rations. The farm could sustain itself by raising most all of its own food in a garden, and with the herds of livestock supplying dairy and meat. With nobody in the family of the right age to join the armed forces, a somewhat normal life continued day by day at the farm.

***

Meanwhile, Cecelia was making the farm house a home. The flowers and particularly, the rose bushes that she planted, came to life each spring adding wonderful rose color and sweet fragrance everywhere around the house.

On the west side of the house she even added flower boxes under the windows, and stuffed them full of Pansies in early spring and later hardier Zinnia that could take the hot summer heat. She started most all the annual flowers from seed inside the house in early spring. The flower boxes made her feel as if she were outside, while she was inside waxing floors or ironing pillow cases. She was most often with a warm smile on her face, even with the bare-bones life she had. Somehow, she could make the best out of just about anything that came her way.

Chapter 5

With a house full of children and adults, Cecelia timed the order of chores, meals and cleaning as a choir director keeps the singers in perfect time to the music. Or even better, like a rowing crew that all have to slice the water at precisely the same time, and at the same depth, in order to keep the boat going straight and steady. We all had our chores to do when we were old enough, whether it was helping around the house with the daily routines, or weeding or picking up twigs in the yard after school. She also let us have play time and seemed to enjoy our games with Trixie or just playing catch ball on the lawn.

Before electricity came to the farm, a summer kitchen was just a few steps from the house door. Inside this oblong building of about ten feet by twenty feet, was a wood-fired stove, similar to the cook-stove in the kitchen. The stove was stuffed with dry hardwood and heated until the burners started to turn red. The hot water steamed from the huge copper-boiler that sat on top of the stove. Cecelia would scoop the hot water out of the boiler with a pail, and pour it into either the claw-foot bath or laundry tubs. Baths were usually, smallest child first, maybe two children at a time. No leisure baths, just in and scrub, wash your hair and out.

The laundry was all done by hand in big tubs, scrubbing on a washboard and rinsing in tub after tub. The clothes washing would most times take all day, and sometimes into the night. In the summer, the clothes were all hung on lines outside. Cecelia would be standing beneath the clothes lines, with two or three wooden pins in her mouth, ready to grab a shirt from the basket below. Sometimes the prairie winds would whip the moisture out of the clothes in just minutes. In the winter months, lines of wet clothes filled the summer kitchen until the next day, when the flame in the wood burner had disappeared, and the coals had turned to ash. The clothes were taken off the lines and brought into the house for folding and pressing.

Twin boy #5 went exploring one day when he was about three years of age, stuck his arm in the near boiling water in the copper boiler that was on the top of the wood-fired stove. He managed 3rd degree burns, so I was told. I remember asking him, when I was older, what had happened to his arm because the skin looked so odd to me. He never really answered me, but one of my older siblings told me what had happened. I am sure, from then on, Cecelia kept a closer watch on the youngest children, to make sure that didn't happen again. Cecelia was very protective of her children, and at the same time, gave us plenty freedom to explore.

When the summer kitchen was in full swing, Cecelia would bring FJ's father outside, and tie his chair to a Boxelder tree so it wouldn't fall over. I have little memory of my grandfather, only that he was almost blind, and Cecelia would care for him and bring him outside to warm in the sun. I also think Cecelia thought he would enjoy the antics of the children on bath day. I don't remember him ever doing anything to help with the children, or with the chores on the farm. He was just old. He slept in the men's room above the kitchen, and one morning he came down the steep steps head first, and that was the last I remember of him. I think he left us in about 1943.

Around that same time, the REA electric lines were finally strung to the rural areas around the county and eventually to the farm. Shortly after that time, the house and barn were hooked up to electric power. The summer kitchen was used year around until the farm house finally added a bathroom off the kitchen with a tub of its own. We still only took baths once a week, now on Saturdays, and had to share the one tub of water with other siblings.

I regretted seeing the summer kitchen abandoned from laundry and baths. It seemed to come to life on those days, the kids running around the yard, sometimes naked, getting ready to jump in the tub for a bath. We had such freedom with Cecelia, she just let us be kids. The building stood vacant for a few years, and the youngest kids used it as a play house, or it was just a kids' hide-a-way.

It wasn't long before FJ decided it would be a good place to store wood for the house-stove, and soon it was full to the door, stacked floor to ceiling, with cords and cords of Ash and any other hardwoods FJ could find.

Chapter 6

The soil in this part of Minnesota is rich and black, unlike the rocky soil about seventy-five miles north. Shortly after Cecelia came to the farm, FJ cleared about an acre of land for a vegetable garden. He plowed and disked until the soil was smooth enough for planting the garden. Even with the relentless hot sun and dry prairie winds, the vegetables flourished with the help of the creek water. Rows of string beans, peas, and many other vegetables brought a new life to the farm and to FJ's life.

By the time fall came, burlap bags filled with root vegetables were hauled down the narrow cellar steps, and placed on a raised wooden crate, to keep the sacks up and off the concrete floor. The cellar was a perfect climate for all the root vegetables such as potatoes, beets and carrots, with a temperature just below forty degrees, and humidity about ninety percent. Soon the cellar shelves were filled with jars of peaches, pears and maybe apricots, if the season was plentiful. Sweet pickles, dill pickles, watermelon pickles and even pork hocks were cured and put into jars. All the stored fruit and vegetables would carry the family through the long winter.

***

When any of the children were old enough to help with harvest in the garden, Cecelia would make it a game for us to help. " If you fill a water glass with raspberries, you can have a glass of cool-aid." "If we pick all the small cucumbers for dill pickles by four o'clock, we can play card games tonight after supper."

***

At times, FJ would bring home crates of seasonal fruits to be canned and stored. Often, the filled canning jars were boiling on the wood fired stove until the wee hours of the night. The girls pealed peaches or skinned pears after Cecelia had dropped the ripe fruit in boiling water, just long enough to loosen the skins. She gently placed the fruit in ice-water to chill, so that the peals would lift easily and not waste any of the fruit. I learned how to use a paring knife in my right hand, and the peach in my left hand, and bring the knife blade towards my thumb and never get cut.

The girls all helped with the assembly line of canning and packing the fruit into jars. Once the lids were on, the jars were placed in a canning kettle and boiled until the lids popped. The popped lids, indicated that the jars were sealed tight. When cooled, they headed to the cellar to be neatly lined up on the shelves. Rows and rows of bright colored raspberries, strawberries, peaches, pears and sometimes cherries were like a masterful work of art in that rather cold and damp cellar. In the fall, as soon as we got home from school, the girls pitched in to help with the canning. The later part of the the summer months, were mostly spent preparing for the long Minnesota winter ahead.

As time went on, the garden grew larger and it well supported the household with most of the food needs year around. Rows of raspberry bushes skirted the west side of the garden with strawberries next in line. Then its was lettuce, carrots, beans, peas and on and on. To the far right, Cecelia planted all the unruly squash, watermelon and cucumbers. These plants seemed to have a mind of their own, and most often trailed where you didn't want them to go. So, they were planted far enough away to not get tangled in the rest of the garden.

The only commercially prepared vegetables we had, were canned peas, whole cornel and cream-style corn from the near-by Green Giant processing plant. Some years the farm raised sweet corn for the Green Giant factory, and in turn FJ could stop by and pick up dented cans of vegetables for next to nothing.

Chapter 7

Again, through the depression years, the farm self-sustained itself. There were at least a dozen milk cows, as many hogs, a pair of plow horses named Tom and Jerry, and a flock of at least one hundred laying chickens. #5 would most often bring the heard of cows into the barn to be milked as the sun was at twilight. Many times, the cows would head back to the barn by themselves, following the bell-weather in single file along their deeply rutted path. They headed to the barn either hungry for the awaiting grain, or that their utters were full and they needed to be milked. I liked to tag along with #5 to the pasture, and on this particular warm summer day, we were walking the cows towards the barn, and #5 said, "Climb under the fence and take the shortcut." I grabbed the wrong barbed wire, the one that was electric, and the current sped through my small body instantly. He saw my dilemma and quickly came to my rescue, pulling me off the hot wire as we both fell over backwards. I knew he felt it too, and I was so thankful he was there. I don't think it is possible to let go by yourself. I didn't tell anyone about what happened. I figured we just took care of it ourselves.

If FJ brought the cows in, he usually had a prod in his hand to move the cattle around and into their stalls. There was very little kindness towards any of the animals, but sometimes I suppose it was necessary to keep them under control.

The cows were milked by hand by the oldest children, sitting on a stool and stripping the milk from the teats into stainless pails. The milk was stored in a separate room connected to the barn. There, the milk was poured into stainless steel milk cans, and the local creamery would come early in the morning to take the cans to the dairy to be processed. Sometimes Cecelia would have the dairy bring a fresh block of cheese, which was a special treat. A milk and cream separator, in the milk house, was used once or twice a week by

Cecelia. She'd pour fresh milk in the top kettle, and crank until the milk would spin fast enough to separate the cream from the milk. Some of the heavy cream was then put in a butter churn, to crank some more, and within a short time, rich creamy butter separated as well. Anything we could make or create ourselves, we did. Very few foods were bought at a store. At one time, I remember we even ground our own wheat flour.

Before electricity, the farm kitchen had an ice-box. FJ would bring blocks of ice home from the ice house in Hutchinson. The ice man would saw ice into blocks out of a near-by lake or the river, and store the blocks inside a big barn-like shed, and cover the ice with sawdust. Usually he could get free sawdust from the local lumber yard, or he could also pack the ice with straw. FJ would clamp an ice tongs around a block of ice, and two or three blocks were set in the ice box, one on top the other. The ice would last up to seven days, even in ninety-degree temperature. You could see right through a block of ice it was so crystal clear. An ice box was common in the 1920s and 1930s, or until electricity came to the rural parts of the state. It seemed short of a miracle, that the tin lined box, could keep milk and cream and whatever needed a chill fresh for that long.

Chapter 8

At one time, Cecelia had White Pekin ducks, and a goose gander or two. She liked seeing the ducks waddling around the yard or swimming in the creek, with their endless following each other and grabbing insects. They were never brought inside a coop in the evening, and soon the flock diminished from a couple of dozen to just a few. Foxes were usually the cause of losing fowl of any kind. A few times during the summer, a fox would jump over or dig under the fence to the chicken coop, and a pile of feathers would be all that was left of a bird in the morning. I don't remember having duck for a meal, so I suspect they were supposed to be just pets. If there were any down feathers around, a few came from ducks, but preferably from a goose, they were saved. The belly of a goose is full of these soft feathers. Cecelia would collect what she could, so she eventually would have enough to make a bed pillow.

Being strong willed, Cecelia announced one day that she was going to have chickens of her own, so she could sell the eggs, and that would be her pocket money. I don't think FJ liked her independence, but that was that. The chickens arrived, and grew up to lay eggs. Once a day she would usually send me, or one of my siblings, out to pick the eggs from under the sitting hens. Hens never wanted to give up the eggs without a fight. A number of chickens would share one nest to lay their daily eggs. Many times, there were at least six or more eggs in one nest each day. The nests were boxes about eighteen inches square, and in a row of about ten wide and piled four or five high. One stubborn hen would want to sit on the freshly laid eggs and not let me take them. I would reach under the white feathers as the pecking started on my hand and arm. Sometimes I wore a glove, but she could peck above on my bare arm. Other times, I would throw a rag over the hen's head, grab her head and neck, and hold it still until I had gathered all the eggs. Freshly laid eggs have a protective coating on the shell to keep away pathogens. We stored the eggs in a steel crate at room temperature on the pantry floor until the crate was full, about eighteen dozen. We washed the eggs just before Cecelia was off to town to sell the crate at the local food store.

In early spring, we would pick up a new batch of baby chickens at the hatchery. I'd like to go along with FJ to the hatchery so I could see the baby chicks breaking out of their shells and coming to life. The chicks were brought home in a box and put in a brooding house with a low quonset shape roof. A small oil heater was placed in the middle of the hut to help keep the young chicks warm. Still, some of the young chicks would smother to death as they huddled in a corner to keep warm. As soon as the weather was warm enough, and the chicks were big enough to scratch around outside, a fenced area was created around the hut, but the chicks were all still shooed-in for the night to escape the predators that hunted during the dark hours. We still seemed to lose a few overnight from maybe a weasel or mink.

As the old chickens stopped laying, they were little by little culled out of the flock. We called these birds stewing hens, as the meat was usually quite tough. A chopping block was just outside the chicken coop, and usually FJ would chop the head off, and watch the headless bird dance around the yard, until the blood was drained out, and the bird would finally collapse. Cecelia had a boiling tub of water ready to scald off the big feathers and later, when the bird's insides were cleaned out, she'd save the liver, gizzard and the heart. Then she would sit on a stump and pull out the remaining pin feathers, and save some of the down type feathers for that future pillow.

Chapter 9

Three meals a day were most often eaten together by the whole family. The kitchen was the most used room in the farm house. It was *also* one of the warmest rooms in the house. Cecelia would be frying pork chops in a cast-iron-skillet, next to a boiling pot of potatoes, while the children were setting the table with plates and silverware. She would open a jar of beets or beans and warm them along-side the pork-chops. The cast-iron cook-top had room for at least four large kettles, and the oven could easily bake two or three cakes at one time. Desserts were common with every evening meal. Sometimes a chocolate cake or just cookies that were baked that day were brought to the table.

After meals, the children pitched in to help clean up the kitchen. First, the plates were scraped and any scraps were put in a dish for the cats or the dog to eat outside. Whatever wasn't food for the cats or dog, went to the pigs. Pigs will eat anything. The dishes were washed and stacked away in the pantry and ready for the next meal. After meals, Cecelia would assign each of us a job and we would rotate each day. One of us would wash the dishes; one would wipe the dishes; one stack the dishes away in the pantry; one would wipe the red oil-cloth covered table and the pantry counter. One swept the kitchen floor and one had to clean the bathroom sink and toilet, the least favorite chore. It was all accomplished without any complaints.

***

It is interesting that most farmers never allowed animals in the house. We weren't any different. The dog and numerous cats were kept outside; cats were for controlling the mice and the dog was a pet, but somewhat of a watch dog to let you know if someone was coming into the farm-yard. These animals always had the barn to escape the cold. The cows gave off enough heat to keep the barn at a comfortable temperature, even in the dead of winter.

***

If there was enough time in the afternoon, Cecelia would often decide to make an angel food cake. She had plenty of eggs from the chickens, and usually it took about a dozen. We'd sit in a circle, maybe three of the girls and Cecelia. We took turns beating egg-whites (one at a time) with a flat whisk until the whites were frothy, adding sugar, little by little until the mixture held a peak on its own. Then a splash of vanilla and continued whipping until Cecelia said it was of a perfect consistency.

Cecelia never measured anything when baking or for that matter, cooking. It was a pinch of salt, a handful of sugar, a sifter full of flour, a shaker of a spice or a spoon full of butter. She just knew when it looked or felt right. She made all her own yeast bread. She'd let the bread rise until the right time to punch it down and let it rise again, and sometimes a third time. When it was *just right*, into the oven it went, and out when perfectly browned. She would say, "Never eat yeast bread when it is warm and fresh out of the oven." "The yeast is still active and will give you a stomach ache."

***

Cecelia did her best to make Christmas as special as possible. Gifts were usually at a minimum, but we always baked sugar cookies to decorate with colored sugars. However, our favorite, was to make taffy. Cecelia would cook the sugar mixture just long enough for a soft boil to hold together when dropped in cold water. Then she would pour the mixture out on the buttered table, and fold it over and over, until it was cool enough to start pulling. Standing a few feet apart, two of us would pull the sugary glob as far apart as we could, fold it back the other way and pull again. Maybe a half hour later, maybe longer, with tired arms, the taffy had gone from a clear liquid to an opaque appearance. While we were pulling the taffy, Cecelia would sometimes add red color to create stripes and add pure peppermint for flavor. When we were finished pulling, we would help cut the taffy into bite size pieces and wrap each piece in wax paper. That sometimes was our Christmas present.

***

The family sat at the table together for each meal. Sometimes we were in a hurry to catch a school bus and little talk took place. But at the evening meal, somehow it most often seemed to be a table lesson. How to eat your soup by scooping the spoon away from you, or a napkin belongs on your lap and is used to wipe your mouth and fingers. Keep your hands on your lap if you are not eating and never put your elbows on the table. Sit up straight and little or no talking by the children, unless you were spoken to. Some of the social etiquette was brought home with #2, when she came back from California for a visit, and was now working at the Sir Francis Drake Hotel in San Francisco.

Meals were family style, and we could dish the food onto our own plates, (when we were old enough) but we had to eat all that we took. No one left the table until everyone was finished. There rarely was much talk between the children. I have often thought about what went through my head at the time, thinking that I (or we) would get a lecture from FJ about something. If I was silent, maybe he wouldn't say anything. The evening meal was his time to get on his soap box, usually about doing more work. I don't think he ever thought children should be children and play and laugh and enjoy growing up. Maybe that is some of the reason we kept silent at meal times.

***

Silence was also a way of life at the parochial school. The nuns did not allow talking while eating, much less in the halls or in the classrooms, unless the teacher asked you to speak.

The nuns almost always assigned homework, and we didn't dare not have it finished for the next day, or we could expect a ruler across our fingers. Sometimes, one of the students, would end up sitting in a corner for maybe half an hour, facing the wall, with a dunce hat on.

Cecelia made sure our homework was finished before we went to bed. I don't remember her ever complaining about the treatment of the children by the nuns. It seems as if the parents gave the teachers authority over the children while they were at school.

***

Saturday was house cleaning day. All the girls were assigned a room in the house to clean. Upstairs, we dusted the little furniture we had, cleaned the window sills and washed the linoleum floors in the bedrooms. The kitchen floor was washed and waxed, and after it was dry, we would use rags or heavy socks to slide across the floor and polish the wax to a high gloss. Everything sparkled when we were finished. Then Cecelia, pretended she was inspecting our work, but never made us do it anything over again.

I remember when Trixie was brought home as a puppy. It was winter and it was too cold for him to be outside; it was the only time that I recall that he was kept inside the house for any length of time. We would take turns polishing the kitchen floor either with big socks or old towels wrapped around our feet. This was another one of Cecelia's way of making a job a game. Trixie caught on to the game really fast, and soon he was sliding with us, and eventually landing head first into the refrigerator. We all rolled on the linoleum laughing along with our new puppy.

Chapter 10

Cecelia's oldest children, were put to work by FJ as soon as they could carry a bucket of milk or handle a broom. They became unpaid working hands as FJ ordered them to shovel, sweep, lift, pull or maybe even crawl to his liking. Cows needed to be milked, pigs slopped, chickens watered and fed, and there was always the perpetual manure to be wheel-barreled outside from the hog-pens or the cow-barn. He seemed to be obsessed with working the step-children to exhaustion. I was told by child #2, that FJ pushed her face into some cow-manure and said, "Eat it, "when she wasn't doing a job to his liking. Cecelia had reached her limit with FJ, with the cruel treatment of her children, and their fights became more frequent. Twin boy #5 was the most defiant, and often the leather strap was used across his back and arms. I remember seeing welts growing on his back as blood came to the surface.

The foul treatment by FJ did not stop #5 from often being in some sort of trouble. In fact, I think it fueled his actions. #5 seemed hard-hearted to just about anyone, and would have a big laugh over most of the outcomes. One time, he loosened the handlebars on his twin sisters' bike, and told her he had just fixed it up for her. "Take it for a ride," he said. Out of the farm yard she went, riding high, standing on the peddles, and down the driveway at full speed. Just before she got to the bridge, the handlebars came off and she careened into the rock pile that bordered the road. She ended up cut, bruised, and quite shaken, and with a broken arm.

In the springtime, the creek would rise like clock-work and flood most of the farm-yard. This time, #5 decided to build a raft out of timbers and planks. He talked his sister into taking it out on its' maiden float. As he pushed the raft from shore, his sister was trying to stand to one side and then the other, as the raft began to sink; eventually to the bottom. #5 got his big laugh in, as his sister stood crying for help.

One winter, with at least a foot of fresh snow, and a beautiful sunny day, #5 decided to hitch up Tom to the stone-bolt, and welcomed as many that wanted a sleigh-ride. We all hopped on, and away we went, flying over snow drifts, bumping over the plowed fields until the sun was starting to sink behind the horizon. #5

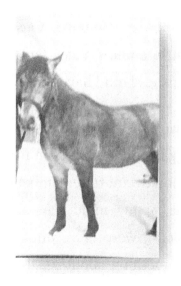

turned Tom's head towards home, and with his last burst of energy, Tom gave the stone-bolt-sleigh a sharp right turn, and we all went flying off into the rough field, including #5. I think #5 was trying to just dump all his passengers off, but instead he was thrown too.

He laughed and laughed as we all gathered ourselves together, a little bruised and achy and full of snow. I think we all thought it was worth it, and laughed with #5. We were close to a mile from home, and had to walk back through the deep snow. It was dark by the time we got to the barn, and Tom was standing by the barn door, waiting to be unhitched. FJ didn't say a word, but we knew what he was thinking. Cecelia always seemed to have a little smile on her face. Maybe she was thinking that she should have come along too.

The worst I remember was when #5 dowsed a pigeon with gasoline and lit it on fire to see how far it could fly. I don't want to remember that time, but it is still so vivid on my mind. As time went on, FJ's strappings of #5 were more often and more severe. There was something about #5 that still drew me to him. I knew he was mischievous and yet he had a way of smoothing things over, like saying, "I have a pack of cigarettes, would you like one?" In the summer, we would sit under the bridge, and smoke a Camel or maybe a Lucky Strike. and then I'd proceed to be sick to my stomach, but never admit it. I guess I just liked to be included when I was small.

One time we were playing in the barn hay-loft. I loved to swing on a rope that we had attached to a big hook on the ceiling. I was swinging with delight, almost the full length of the barn. Then, the rope slid through my hands at the far end, and I slid down next to the barn wall. I was way over my head in hay, and couldn't get out by myself. #5 came to my rescue and dropped a rope down for me to grab onto, as he pulled me out of the hole.

***

With her egg money, Cecelia would sometimes take us to the movie theater for a Saturday afternoon matinee. The small-town theater would often have Roy Rogers western showing, with a Micky Mouse Cartoon and a News Reel. But, sometimes it would be a little more of an adult movie, and when I would sit next to Cecelia, and it wasn't what she thought I should see, (like two people kissing,) she would cover my eyes and tell me not to look. #5 would say, "You better keep your feet up or the rats will crawl up your legs." I kept my feet off the floor, as I hung on to the seat cushion with the gum plastered on the seats' underside.

There was a small store next to the theater, and when Cecelia wasn't with us, #5 would send me inside with a note and a quarter to buy a pack of cigarettes. He had written a note that the cigarettes were for my mother. The clerk handed over the pack without any questions.

At the farm, the garden was across the driveway bridge, and #5 would send me out to pick something for Cecelia; maybe some tomatoes or squash. And as I am starting by the rock piles on the side of the road he would yell, "Better hurry on or a weasel will come out of the rocks and bite into your leg and suck all the blood out of you."

We had neighbors directly across the township road from us, and late in the day, Cecelia and the kids would sometimes sit outside on their porch to watch the sunset. After dark, we would walk home through the thick   woods, and we could hear the leaves wrestling as nocturnal hunters were moving around. #5 would yell out, "You better run fast, there are bears hiding in the woods and they will eat you up."

Chapter 11

Neighbors are the life-blood of the rural communities. The farmers seem to all share and care for each other when sick or in need of food or just about anything. Most of the roads around the farm land follow the section lines that are six hundred forty acres; a square mile. A neighbor is usually within a mile or less depending how large your farm is. FJ had only one hundred sixty acres, so some of the neighbors were much closer. Evenings were often spent at a neighbor's house, kids playing games and parents talking about the wind or rain or how the crops were progressing. Because Cecelia knew the neighbors well, and knew that she was welcome any time of day or night, she would often take refuge from FJ's abuse by showing up on one or the other's doorstep, afraid to go back home to another beating. I was told she would run barefoot down the gravel road to a close-by farm, too afraid to waste time finding shoes. FJ was the silent abuser. He was very careful to limit his hitting or dragging Cecelia by her hair to mostly when the children were not at home.

***

My earliest recollection, I suppose when I was about two or so years old. Cecelia was playing with me on the bed that was hers and FJ's. He came into the bedroom and told her to "get that kid out of here." He picked me up and tossed me into the crib that was in the same room. I don't remember what happened after that, but it wasn't long before the room was changed back into a sitting room, and Cecelia put a bed upstairs in the open space at the top of the steps for herself. From then on, FJ occupied the men's room that was directly above the kitchen, with #5 and #7. Life went on after that, but with an intensity in the air that is hard to describe. There was very little interaction between FJ and Cecelia when any of the children were around. I suppose most of the fighting took place when we were at school.

Chapter 12

The R.E.A. (Rural Electric Association) was established in 1935, and at last the miracle energy was reaching more rural areas. The lines were finally strung to the farm shortly after #8 was born, about 1941. A washing machine from Sears Roebuck with a ringer to squeeze the water out of the clothes came into the kitchen shortly thereafter. The clothes still occupied the living room to dry on Mondays, but the manual labor of washing was now mostly done by the machine.

The Amana electric stove with four burners on top, and an oven with a temperature gauge on the front, also found a home in the kitchen. It did take some of the temperature guessing away from Cecelia, but I doubt if she paid very much attention to the gauge anyway. The daily and weekly chores were suddenly much easier for Cecelia and for the children as well.

Chapter 13

Cecelia was an accomplished seamstress, and many nights the foot trundle of the Singer Sewing Machine would be racing through the night. She made most all of her own clothes and the children's clothes as well. Hand-me-downs were just the way it was for the children. I don't think the youngest ever saw anything new. Many of the fabrics she used were from flour sacks that came in many small prints and check patterns that are still copied today. They were all one hundred percent cottons, that washed up beautifully and could be made into a skirt or a dress or a nightgown or even underwear. Other farmers would give her the empty sacks if they had more than they needed.

All the children were dressed neat and clean whether going to school or to church. One of my favorite sayings of Cecelia's was, "You may have an excuse for being poor, but not one for being dirty."

Cecelia and several of the neighbors started a sewing bee. Some of the women were working on

patch-work-quilts, and some embroidering dish towels and pillow cases or just mending holes in socks and whatever needed repair. Cecelia would often be mending socks but also started crocheting, weaving many doilies to place on the sofa arms, or the chair back to lay your head on. The conversations were much like today, when a bunch of girls get together, and talk about raising children or how to solve a conflict or to share a new recipe. Her friends knew she was becoming more and more afraid of FJ. Sometimes they would notice a bruise or part of her hair looking unruly.

***

Monday was always wash day, and in the winter, clothes-lines were strung across the living room to dry the wet clothes. In summer, after the bed sheets had whipped by the prairie winds, they were brought in, and still maybe steam pressed before going back on each bed. We didn't have a steam iron, so we wetted a towel and ironed through it to take out the few wrinkles. Most everything was ironed that was flat cotton and with this many children, the ironing board was never stored away, it stood in the sitting room (X bedroom) off the living room. All the girls took turns ironing. The bed- sheets that were hung outside had that sweet smell of the wind; at least for the first night.

Chapter 14

Late summer and into the early fall were the best times of year to live on the farm. The neighbors, five or six farms, would get together and all help each other with the harvest of small grains such as wheat and oats and sometimes barley. The big threshing machine would roll into the yard pulled by an iron-cog-wheeled Case tractor. The grain bundles, had been leaned into each other to dry (a shock) for maybe a week before the threshing started. Once fed into the thresher, in a matter of a minute, the grain flew out of a chute and dropped into a trailer while the straw blew high in the sky to form a hay stack. The chaff from the milling was thick in the air, making it sometimes hard to breathe, but it smelled so sweet and fresh. The farm cattle could not get along without the straw for bedding down in the barn. Straw has hollow stems and it doesn't absorb moisture.

While the machines were purring in the fields, the women were busy preparing pies, cakes and noon and late day meals. Cecelia and the other women were so well organized. Roast beef was in the oven while a volume of potatoes were cooking on the cast-iron stove-top. Vegetables were in abundance from the gardens as well as fruit for pies. Tables were set up outside on the lawns and the workers sat in the shade whenever possible. The crowd of about two dozen adults were well fed, and often worked until the dew set on the grain in the fields. The beverages were kept cold in a cattle watering tub with an ice block that lasted all day in the shade. A beer or two was an expected treat for the male workers at the end of the day.

The children of all the families came along to the grain threshing. In fact, children seemed to always come with the parents to everything. They delighted in hiding inside the freshly blown haystacks and sliding down the bins full of fresh grain. The harvest was a grand time for playing hide and seek. Sometimes we would deliver a watered-down beer to the operator of the thresher. We would either drink or pour out half the beer from a bottle, and fill it up with water, and wait to see if the threshing machine operator (MK) noticed. " The beer isn't what it used to be," he'd say. We giggled from behind a grain wagon as we enjoyed the success of our joke. One time we found a Kentucky Bourbon bottle buried in a grain bin, but thought better of taking it. Best we stay out of that trouble, not knowing who it belonged to. The farms that participated in the harvest were not close enough to each other to have frequent friends over to play, so this was an annual time that the children looked forward to as well as the adults.

One time, I road along with one of the bachelor neighbors who lived with his mother longer than anyone should. He was a tall skinny guy in his late thirties, with a greyish complexion. He never really looked anyone in the eye. We were pulling a grain cart from the field and I was sitting sort of on his lap on the tractor's seat. The next thing I knew, he had his hand between my legs and I froze. It didn't take me long to jump off the tractor and take a short-cut across the field, heading for home. I remember one time I was waiting with one of the nuns at school, someone was going to pick me up because I had missed the bus. The nun said to sit on her lap and then her words were, "Never let a man touch you down here," as she patted between my legs. I think she was prepping me for the convent life. Sometimes I would be in the same place as the skinny guy, and I would just make sure I was a safe distance away from him. I wondered if he ever remembered the time on the tractor, or if he just wasn't right upstairs. I didn't tell Cecelia and certainly not FJ about the skinny guy or the nun. It seemed like I just grew up taking care of myself, and not running back to tattle for whatever the reason.

In May of 1945, FJ came home and stated: "The war was over and Hitler was dead." Somehow I thought everything would get better at home for everyone.

When any of the children were of school age, Cecelia enrolled them in Saint Boniface Catholic School. It was good that we all wore uniforms so that everyone looked the same. There really weren't any rich people around, but some were much better off than we were, and some were scraping for a living and on public assistance.

On my first day of school, kindergarten, I didn't like it there and ran away (across the street) to a house where the lady was a friend of my mother. She called Cecelia. She came and picked me up in the late afternoon and didn't say much. I guess it was OK not to like it at school. The next morning, I was back riding the bus with my siblings. This time, Cecelia told me that I had to stay at school the whole day. And, that was that.

***

By the time I started school, #1 was already a senior in high school, and left the farm as soon as she graduated and headed for the city to find a job. #2 was already living with a doctor's family in Hutchinson, and graduated High School from there. She left for Minneapolis shortly thereafter, and then on to San Francisco. Cecelia wrote and begged the California Joe W. to send for the twins, #4 and #5. They would be ready to start public high school in the fall, and #5 was becoming more difficult as the days went on. That summer, California Joe W. sent two tickets for the Great Northern Railway, and boy #5 was off to California to live with his recluse father. His twin sister didn't follow until the next year.

Chapter 15

When #1 and #2 were first working girls in the Twin Cities, they took Cecelia on a vacation to Wisconsin Dells. They were gone for a long weekend, but it must have seemed like forever for Cecelia. It was the first time she had ever left Minnesota. I just look at her with a big smile on her face, next to those two rather charming, strapping young men. I suppose she was happy to be away from the farm, happy to be on a boat, happy to be with her two oldest daughters and happy not be slaving away from morning until night.

Chapter 16

Cecelia made sure the last three children, (FJ's) went to the dentist and doctor as often as she could financially arrange. FJ never wanted to spend money on anything *he* didn't think was necessary, and maybe it was also because Cecelia insisted on doctor and dentist. At that time, all the disease prevention shots were given at school by the county nurse. # 6, # 7 and # 8 had their tonsils and adenoids taken out all at the same time at the Hutchinson hospital. I am not sure why, except someone thought this would prevent sickness, and these were useless body parts we didn't need anymore. It must have been cheaper for the three of us to have the operations all at one time. #6 got an infection and needed more attention than #7 and #8. However, we all enjoyed as much homemade ice cream as our tummies could hold. Cecelia started with the rich cream that she had spun off from the fresh milk; added some sugar, a little salt and maybe vanilla, raspberries or strawberries. She turned the crank on the churn for twenty to thirty minutes, then into the freezer for a few hours and, Walla! Delicious ice cream.

***

One winter evening, I was trying to run up the steep steps with #6 chasing me around the house, playing a game of some sort. When I got to the top step, I tripped and slid smack into an iron bed-frame. I caught the outside of my left eye and it began bleeding profusely. Cecelia did her best to stop the bleeding with cold presses, and asked FJ to take me to the doctor. He refused. Eventually I healed with a scar about a half inch long just below my eye. Lucky I didn't hit any higher or my eye sight may have been compromised.

Another time, I tore my ankle open on barb-wire that was buried in some tall grass. Cecelia bandaged me up and once again, no doctor. I still have a long scar as a reminder.

***

Nobody went to the dentist for cleaning at that time; you were expected to keep your own teeth clean at home with baking soda straight out of the box. We all had our wisdom teeth removed, however, not at the same time. The dentist said they were unnecessary teeth that usually caused problems and would be in the way.

We used an abundance of apple cider vinegar for just about any ailment we had, whether it was a tooth ache, tummy ache, sore throat, hiccups and even to get rid of dandruff.

***

Cecelia would take #6, #7, and #8 along to town whenever possible. Our biggest treat was to eat a hamburger at Yanishacks Restaurant. She'd lift me up on the black and white swivel stools next to the colorless Formica counter with the metal edge. The counter was long an skinny with at least 20 stools. From anywhere in town, we knew we were close to the hamburger joint; we could smell the onions frying for blocks away. If I think about it, I can still taste that burger with three slices of dill pickles, a pile of fried onions and a squirt of catsup, on a soft white bun, and presented on a sheet of waxed paper. It was delicious.

Cecelia was always very cautious about just about everything. "Hang on to the counter so you don't fall off the stool." "Hold each other's hand when you cross the street."

Cecelia was also very superstitious. We heard about black cats crossing your path being bad luck; broken mirrors can't stay; tossing salt over your left shoulder for good luck; Friday the 13th and all the other thirteens to stay away from. "Don't walk under that ladder, it is bad luck." "Be careful of the cracks in the sidewalk, it is the path to evil below." I remember playing with an umbrella one time at home, and as I started to open it inside the house, she snatched it away and said, "That would anger the gods." We also had a horseshoe over the barn door and we never had any black cats on the farm. And, a Saint Christopher medal usually road along with us in the car.

Seven of Cecelia's children that lived on the farm, all dressed to go to church.

Chapter 17

The winters were brutal in the farm house. One of the only places that seemed to be warm was by the kerosene heater in the living-room. Some of that heat would make its way upstairs through the register to the bedroom above. FJ kept the old wood-fired cookstove fired up to heat the kitchen and the stairway, and some of that warmth made its way to the men's bedroom above the kitchen. Sometimes, the three youngest would huddle around the upstairs register above the kerosene stove, put a blanket over their heads to trap the heat, and play a game, usually Monopoly. Chinese Checkers was another favorite, but the marbles kept falling through the register, and sometimes into the heater below, lost forever in the soot and fire. Another way we kept warm, was to open the oven door of the wood fired stove, and put our feet inside, until our socks were steaming.

It seemed that so often we would be huddled together, just to feel each other's body heat. I remember one night I was sitting close to Cecelia on the blue velvet sofa, and she was brushing my hair and talking about school and the nuns, and just about nothing and everything. Then she said, "I may not be around much longer, and I worry about you, because you are so young." I didn't know what to think about what she said at the time. Those words have always stayed with me.

***

Cecelia loved music, and as time went on, we had several 78 records. We'd sing along with Perry Como, Hank Williams and even Hank Snow. We could occasionally get a scratchy radio station that would also play some of our favorites, but most times we relied on phonograph records. We'd sit in a circle on the living room floor, and sing along with Hank or Perry. I think it also kept us warm on those cold winter nights. Twin girl #6 taught herself to strum the guitar, and she could play all the right cords along with the songs on the 78s.

She had a wonderful voice, and could yodel with the best of the country singers.

FJ also had a love for music, although he never said too much about it, nor did he join in our singing parties. Before Cecelia came to the farm, FJ was part of a German dance band that played in the local dance halls. Sometimes when we would come in the house or just home from school, and FJ was in the house alone, we could hear the polka music blaring from the radio. Somehow, a piano made its way into the sitting room off the living room. FJ never had a music lesson, but he could cord along on the piano with ease. I'm guessing someone either gave FJ the old upright, or he bartered for it. The small instruments that FJ also played, were all stored in the attic with an access door at the top of the stairs. A set of orchestra bells, a trumpet, a trombone, a flute and a clarinet were all catching dust. I never heard FJ play any of the attic instruments. I would like to visit them every now and then just to feel the smooth shiny brass, and I wondered how hard they would be to play.

Our winter evenings on the farm were often spent playing cards around the kitchen table. Cecelia would join in with the children and we would play Canasta or Gin-Rummy until bedtime. All the children were included, no matter how small you were.

One Christmas, we all received ice skates for presents. My skates had two runner blades. I was maybe four years old. That night, the moon was full as we walked to Whitney Lake, less than a half mile away. We were so used to walking wherever we wanted to go, that the distance seemed like nothing. The air was brisk and the lake was frozen solid with patches of ice and snow all mixed up in beautiful patterns. We could skirt around a copse of trees or just spin and speed to our hearts' content. My older siblings held my hands until I was steady enough on my double blades to skate on my own. We skated until the moon dropped down below the horizon. When we got back home, Cecelia had hot chocolate waiting for us. We were tired and a little cold, with rosy cheeks and red noses and big smiles for that most perfect night at Whitney Lake.

Chapter 18

I can still envision Cecelia, in the heat of the summer, packing up the three youngest and off to Lake Eagle we would go, about a mile from the farm. She had a Red Flyer Wagon with food, towels and blankets that she pulled along, so if one of us got tired we could ride for a bit, #6, #7 and #8. The lake was in a farmer's cow pasture, and we would climb under the barb-wire fence and follow the cow path down to the lakes edge, where a couple of big shade trees swayed in the wind; the perfect place for Cecelia to sit and watch us paddle around in the lake. The lake bottom was sandy with a gentle grade. There was a barrel out in the water that we could climb up on and jump and splash until we were hungry or too tired and had to retreat back to shore. Cecelia always brought some salt along for the blood suckers that lived on the barrel. A little shake of salt and suckers would lose their grip and slither off our legs or arms.

We also would pile in the car and go to Lake Marion, where Cecelia would once again bring the towels and a blanket and radish or lettuce sandwiches and a jar of cool-aid. We would spend most of the afternoon swimming and just playing in the water. We all had taken swimming lessons, first at the scary river dam in Hutchinson, and then at Lake Marion.

The Lake Marion Beach had a diving raft, so we could swim to the raft and dive or jump off to our hearts content. By late afternoon we were usually very tired and terribly sunburned. It was time to head home.

We had to be back to the farm in time to make supper. On those stifling summer evenings, we dreaded trying to sleep in the upstairs bedroom. Once or twice a summer we would ask Cecelia if we could use a blanket or a bed sheet to toss over the wash-line and form a tent. Somehow we secured the ends to keep the bugs out, maybe safety-pins, and used rocks from the creek to hold down the sides of the blanket. I don't know if it was any cooler inside our home-made tent, but it was somewhat of a game to see if we could stay there all night. Most times we did.

Chapter 19

It was one of the hottest days and nights of the summer in mid-July. Dr. Spock was giving new parents advise in his *Common-Sense Book on Baby and Child Care* while in Nuremberg, Nazi leaders are scheduled to be hanged for *crimes against humanity* within the year.

The air was suffocating. Shortly before midnight, the wind started to pick up, and within a very short time, Cecelia was calling for us to come down in the cellar, a big storm was coming. Half asleep, we crawled down the steep-cellar-ladder and shut the heavy lid behind the last one down. We huddled together in the dampness, next to the remaining jars of canned peaches and pork hocks, left over from last winter. The wind howled and the lightning flashed through the small window on the east end of the cellar. "Not to worry, we will be alright. It is safe down here," said Cecelia. We heard trees cracking and objects being thrown around outside, sometimes banging against the house. The storm didn't last very long, maybe twenty minutes or so. Then it was dead quiet. The electricity was out, but when we climbed back out of the cellar, the moon was shining brightly enough to see some of the results of the storm. The house was intact, but the chicken brooding house had sailed in the air and landed close to the house, still upright. The corn crib was laying on its side. Shingles had blown off the barn, but otherwise the buildings seemed to be alright. The trees were the biggest loss. The driveway was littered with downed trees, big and small. All along the creek huge cottonwoods were uprooted. At first I thought it was a building blown over, but one of the biggest trees along the creek had been yanked up by the roots. It could have been a tornado, or maybe it was just a bad storm. We were all sad about the trees, the creek would never be the same again. Cecelia and I had often been able to find a shady spot under a big cottonwood, sit on a big bolder and stretch our toes into the cool water on one of the many hot and humid mid-summer days. That would never happen quite the same again.

The next morning, neighbors came to help clear the trees from the driveway, so that we could at the least get in and out. It took weeks to gather all the brush and pile it up to eventually be burned. The farmstead looked so barren without the trees. Cecelia had a big project ahead of her. Knowing her, she would have the yard shaped up again in no time at all.

Chapter 20

It was the summer of 1949, and Cecelia had had enough of the mistreatment from FJ. She loaded the three of us in the car, and off we went to the McLeod County Court House in Glencoe, in hopes that the court could do something about her abuse from FJ. Although I don't remember FJ ever physically abusing any of his three children, but he had a violence about him, and who was to say that he wouldn't turn on his own, as he did on the step-children. I think we went to an office that is somewhat like our Child Protection today. The three of us, # 6, #7 and #8, sat on a cold granite bench in the hallway of the court house while Cecelia pleaded her case. When she came out of the chamber, she had a piece to paper that said something about FJ was supposed to leave her and the children alone.

FJ seemed to abide by the ruling for a period of time, maybe a few months. The house was very quiet.

Chapter 21

There were three fires at the farm that I recall. The wood cook-stove in the kitchen that still served as heat in the winter, had an exposed stove pipe that came up out of the stove, across the ceiling for about six feet, and another right turn for another few feet, and then into the chimney. There were four right angles to get to the chimney. On more than one occasion, the stove pipe would start to smell of hot metal and FJ would ease up on stoking the stove's fire with more wood. Most likely, the wood was not dry enough and pitch was building up inside the stove pipes. The first fire was when the pipe was so red hot, that it split apart and was burning inside. The fire department came and helped put the stove-pipe and chimney fire out with minor repair.

The second fire was in late fall. Everyone on the bus was gawking at our house as the school bus stopped at the end of the driveway. The tanker-fire-truck was shooting water up and into the roof, with flames licking at the shingles around the hole. The attic was obviously on fire. The fire department was able to get the blaze under control just as the sun was setting. Neighbors helped FJ patch the roof temporarily as winter was on the horizon. The roof was more permanently repaired in the spring, but the attic and all those instruments appeared to be a lost cause.

I leaned a ladder up to the attic one time after that fire to see about the musical instruments that were lying in the ash and charred joists. They were ruined. I wondered why no one cared about them after the fire. I also wondered why none of the children were ever encouraged to play any of those beautiful instruments?

I climbed the stairs every night up to the girl's bedroom and brushed by the brick chimney, feeling the heat radiate from the hot bricks, wondering if this would be another fire. I guess we were always working on staying warm, so the hot bricks were quite welcome.

Chapter 22

By the summer of 1950, America was once again at war, sending troops to South Korea in their battle against the North. Cecelia had her own battles on the home front that summer. And again, her fear of FJ landed us back at the court house pleading for help to get far away from him. Most of the battles between them must have taken place while we were at school – he seemed to be on his good behavior when the children were at home. We were sitting on the same granite bench at the McLeod County Court House, when Cecelia came out with news that we were moving to Little Falls. I don't remember if she took the only farm car, or if some of her relatives from her first marriage picked us up in Glencoe. Someone in Little Falls was contacted and made arrangements for a place for us to live that was within walking distance from the Catholic School. Cecelia kept in close touch with Joe W's family, as daughter #3 was living close by with her aunt. I don't know for sure, but I am guessing they were the ones to help us get settled in Little Falls.

The house was a two-story clap-board house with big square rooms and a front porch the width of the house. Stately oak trees hung close over the roof and kept the house shaded from the hot afternoon sun. Cecelia rented the main floor, furnished with the necessities, and better than she had at the farm. She somehow got a job as a housekeeper for a family in Little Falls. We started school in September, just after the fall classes began. We seemed to fit in ok. We wore uniforms like we did in our last school, so everyone looked alike. I remember being introduced to the class on my first day in fifth grade. The nuns seemed to be very understanding and didn't ask any questions. I don't remember making many friends to play with after school, but there were plenty of activities at school to keep us busy. It was nice to be able to walk home from school and not have to ride the bus and be met with the endless work duties at the farm. But, I did miss our dog, Trixie. Our faithful black and white terrier would meet the school bus every day, summer or winter, and play hide and seek until we were all too tired to hide anymore.

A month or two went by, and we were settled into a peaceful routine in Little Falls. Most times Cecelia was back at the house when we returned home from school, and everything seemed to be going as good as could be expected. Then, in late fall, FJ started showing up at school to see us, sometimes weekly. We would be lured out of the classroom by a nun and told that "our dad was here to see us." We were brought to an office where he would plead or try to bribe us to come back to the farm. He would slip a (Montana) silver dollar in each one of our hands in hopes that this would sway our decision as to whether we would return to the farm. None of the three of us gave him an answer.

It wasn't until early December of that year, when Cecelia gathered the three of us together, and gave us a choice of what we wanted to do. She said that she had lost her job as a housekeeper, and that Christmas was coming, and she would not be able to buy us anything this year. FJ had said he wanted us all back at the farm and he would make sure we had a nice Christmas. I am not sure if we really made the choice, or if she encouraged us to go. We thought we were all going, and as it was, FJ came to pick us up, and Cecelia stayed behind.

Christmas came and went with very little memory of it. After all, without Cecelia, it was a house without a spirit. It was late January when she finally came back to the farm. We saw very little of her as she stayed in bed most of the time. We had gone back to the Parochial school as if nothing had ever happened. I don't remember anyone ever asking any questions about where we had been for four months, or maybe I just blocked that out of my memory. Once again, we were back to a somewhat normal routine.

Chapter 23

The last time I saw Cecelia, was the morning of February 23rd, 1951. We were up out of bed, and getting dressed for school, about 7:00am. Just as I was coming down the steps, the sweet aroma of hot oatmeal filtered into my senses. I was so happy to see Cecelia up and around, and what seemed to be her usual cheerful self. I finished breakfast and put my coat on along with my other siblings. We headed out the door and down the driveway to meet the bus about 7:30. Everything seemed like it was going to be back to what we were used to with Cecelia.

It was early afternoon, when one of the nuns called the three of us out of our classrooms. She told us that there had been a fire at our farm, and we were to take a different bus, and go to a neighbor's farm after school, that was a few miles south of where we lived. We didn't think this was too unusual as we had had fires at the farm before. At our friend's house, we played our usual games of hide and seek and a late-night game of monopoly.

It was early the next morning when FJ came by the farm where we spent the night, and we heard him talking downstairs. The next thing I remembered, he opened the door at the bottom of the stairs, and we were all looking down on him from the top of the steps. He had tears in his eyes and said, "Your mother is dead." I couldn't believe what he was saying. I just saw her the morning before and she was fine.

We stayed at the neighbors for another night, and reluctantly went back to our farm. By the time her death reached the news, I remember sitting on the blue velvet sofa with my siblings, and Cedric Adams was on WCCO radio announcing about the tragic suicide of a woman, who left 8 children orphaned, one as young as ten years old. And, added, "How could she do a thing like that?" I, wondered too.

The Catholics, at least at that time, have a wake or a deathwatch, for three days the body is at home for friends to stop by and pay their last respect. I was told the priest came and gave her, what is referred to as the last sacraments, before she died. That is supposed to remove her sins and help her into heaven. Her closed casket was placed where the blue velvet sofa had been for so many years. That was her favorite place to sit in the evening and spend time with the children. It seemed right to be placed there. Those three days seemed like an eternity, with well-wishers traipsing in the house, bringing food and offering what sympathy they could. The bathroom, where she apparently died, was closed off to everyone. We still had an outhouse out back, so we didn't need to go in there.

The morning she died, as FJ tells it, he was out doing chores, and saw smoke coming from the house and came to see what was wrong. He said Cecelia had started a fire in the bathroom and he said he found her outside the front door of the house. He said he picked her up and brought her back inside, that was about nine a.m. She died about noon that day.

The walls and woodwork were burned black and large area on the linoleum floor was burned. Numerous matches were found in the bathtub, burned and unburned. The county coroner stated that, "The burns were self-inflicted. And, that she had been in ill health for several months." I wondered how he knew that?

Most of the siblings were at the funeral except twin boy #5. His father wouldn't spend the money to send him back to Minnesota. Seven of us were lined up like birds on a wire as the priest said some boiler-plate niceties about our mother. I remember looking up at sister #1 and she was crying so hard all through the Catholic Mass of the Dead. I think I was in shock, because for some reason I couldn't cry at the church. Being I went to the church's school next door, we often sang at funerals. I suddenly realized how sad they were. When the service was over, we went to the cemetery where FJ had arranged a grave site for Cecelia and for himself, eventually. It all seemed like a dream or a nightmare. It couldn't be true that she was never coming home.

Chapter 24

From then on, there was a dark cloud of emptiness that hung over the farm. FJ said less than he ever had in the past. His routine didn't change, but he expected his children that were at home to take over the duties of their mother, like nothing ever happened. Besides going to school full time, #7 worked outside with FJ, taking care of the animals etc., while #6 and #8 were suddenly in charge of taking care of the house, which included cooking all the meals, washing clothes, ironing, cleaning etc. etc. We had to give up being kids and were suddenly thrown into the role of being adults. I often wondered if FJ ever thought about us not being able to be kids anymore? Nobody came by to see if we were ok, that I recall. We didn't have time to have a friend over, and just maybe, the parents didn't want their children around FJ. Although he was never physically abusive to his three children, he also never showed any love. Not a hug or kiss or compliment; just orders. Even on Saturday, the only day we could sleep-in, FJ would yell up the steps in his braying voice, about 6:00am and say, "It is time to get up." If he was up, everyone was up. One time when I complained, or maybe made a comment about something he was demanding, he started to say, "You are just like your M........, and then stopped. I knew what he meant.

***

For months after Cecelia's death, the county sheriff would come by unannounced and ask FJ to come with him to his office; he had some additional questions he would like answered. I remember him coming a few times, but it may have been far more often, most likely, when the kids were all at school. The questioning went on for at least a year, and maybe more like two years. Then the sheriff stopped coming. He apparently had to either charge FJ or leave him alone.

One day, shortly after that time, I don't know exactly what I was looking for in the cellar, but I spotted a roll of papers stuck up in the rafters above where the well-water came into the house. It was a thick roll of aged parchment paper. I began to read over each page of question after question about what exactly happened the day Cecelia died. I told #7 about the papers that I had found, and we went to look for them again within a few days, and they were gone. We were afraid FJ knew we found the inquest papers, so he had to destroy them. He must have demanded the questioning files from the sheriff's office being they weren't charging him with a crime.

I have no idea how he was able to get the files from the sheriffs' office, maybe a bribe of some sort. Sixty years later, there was a box with Cecelia's name on it labeled – Investigation Files Under Court Seal. And, it was empty. FJ insisted that he saw smoke coming from the house while he was doing chores, ran to the door and found Cecelia outside. He said he carried her inside the house and placed her on the living room floor. She died about three hours later from what the coroner said were "self-inflicted burns." A certificate of death by suicide was completed by the deputy coroner. There must have been questions about her death at the time because a second coroner was called to the scene from another town. The county sheriff at the time apparently did not believe FJ's story, but did not have enough evidence to charge him. The sheriff continued his questioning as long as he could, and I guess he just ran into a dead-end, with no witnesses at the scene at the time of Cecelia's death.

***

More often than not, when people are closing in on their last days, they need to get grating issues off their chest. The neighbor was asked by FJ to come and repair the bathroom. I don't know if FJ didn't want to do it himself or if he didn't have the talent or desire to do a repair. And, now that the sheriff was finally leaving him alone, he could officially remove any potential evidence. While the neighbor is repairing the bathroom, it looked very strange to him, and appeared as if the bathroom door was being held shut by someone on the outside. There were handprints on the door and casing that showed a struggle. I am guessing the sheriff noticed the same thing, and that was why FJ was brought in for questioning so many times.

The neighbor stated to a family member that FJ should have been put away a long time ago for his treatment of Cecelia. So often she had come to his house crying and scared that FJ was going to kill her. The neighbor died shortly afterward. With all the neighbors who knew about the abuse and horrible goings on at the farm, no one ever confided with any of the children, and as a matter of fact, I never heard any whispers or talk about FJ and Cecelia, not until decades later. I suppose they thought it was better to leave the words unsaid, and maybe the children would be less affected by it all. *It was all those things everyone thought, but did not say.* Maybe they were right. Maybe they were also afraid of FJ.

After FJ had died, there was a gathering at the farm of many of Cecelia's church and neighbor friends. #2 was visiting from California and the friends were brought together for her. As soon as we walked in the door, one of the close neighbors stood up and said, "He killed her you know, he killed her and should have been locked up for what he did." Other heads nodded in agreement. It was a somber moment for me. I hadn't realized how vivid Cecelia was still so fresh on the minds, this was thirty-five years later.

Chapter 25

It wasn't long before FJ started selling all the farm animals. I think there was one horse left and it went to what they called *the glue factory*. The Holstein herd of milk cows were either sold to other farmers with the balance trucked to the cattle auction. At least a dozen swine were also taken to market. The chickens were the last to leave, and now the farm was depleted of animals except for a few cats and Trixie. And, that beautiful and abundant garden, was now a patch of weeds. This all happened in about a year or two after Cecelia died.

After that, the land was filed into soil bank, and FJ sold whatever machinery that had any value. He never was much of a farmer – he didn't like physical work. For about a dozen years he had child labor doing most all of the farm work.

Barren of animals, FJ had a lot of free time to read and practice his penmanship. The St. Paul Pioneer Press would come each morning, and he would proceed to read it cover to cover, and then fill the margins with a's and b's etc., etc., until all the margins were filled with beautiful circles of letters.

FJ often went hunting and fishing whenever he chose; even trips to Montana for elk hunting. He made his annual deer hunting trip to northern Minnesota and always came home with a kill. He was an excellent marksman and a big buck was usually tied to the roof of the car as he pulled into the yard. We would have to eat deer sausage, and venison steaks and hamburger for the next few months. He was the only one that liked the deer meat.

He also started traveling on buses and trains, often leaving us for a week or two while he visited national parks and famous sites around the US. He would bring home boxes full of color slides, and he would tell us he was going to show us his latest adventures. He liked history, and would tell us the height of every mountain and the depth and length of rivers. Then he would spend his time planning his next trip.

Chapter 26

When we left Little Falls, just before Christmas of the previous year, Cecelia did not come with us. I didn't know what to think at the time except that she did not want to go back to live with FJ. Some sixty years later, when I am at the funeral of #3, the child that lived with her aunt, it all comes into focus why she didn't come back with us to the farm.

Cecelia had gone to stay with her first husband's relatives once again. She told them that she had been raped by the man that she worked for in Little Falls and found herself pregnant. When she told us that she lost her job, it was because not only was she pregnant, but her belly was growing. When FJ saw her that morning, she had to confess her condition. *She had no way out.*

And, what happened then? Is it possible that FJ came in the house with the can of kerosene, for the living room stove, as part of his morning chores? That is what he usually did. He found Cecelia finally up out of bed and in the kitchen. She tried to escape into the bathroom and FJ held the door, splashed some kerosene and lit the fatal matches. A container of wooden matches hung on the wall to the left of the bathroom door. To get a flame, you had to strike the matches on the side of the box or on the stove to the right of the door. Could Cecelia have done this by herself?

I imagine, FJ could not get over that she didn't want anything to do with him, and yet, here she is pregnant with another man's baby. Finally, the mental anger turned to rage, and there was no turning back.

I wish the sheriff had known what led up to the horrific events of that day, rather than relying on FJ's words about what happened.

If Cecelia was going to commit suicide, why would she come all the way back to the farm to take her own life?

In the papers that I had read as a child, I remember how FJ answered the same questions by the county sheriff over and over, exactly the same way. He probably began to believed it himself.

Coroners from two different towns came to the farm to try to determine the *Cause of Death*. If obviously was not an easy stamp for them to put on Cecelia's death certificate.

Chapter 27

So often I have been with friends that are taking their mothers somewhere; maybe even pushing a wheel chair or manning a walker. I just say to myself, "lucky you." I still wonder what it would have been like to have Cecelia for a more normal lifetime. They say time heals it all, and maybe that is somewhat true; the emptiness does eventually fade; but some memories never vanish like you might want them to; the ones that cut deep into your soul. They just become invisible.

On the brighter side, Cecelia will always be young and vibrant to me. I never saw her ill, or old, or in a care facility. I can look at the pictures of her and see a warm, cheerful woman who cared for all of us in the best way she possibly could.

From that day on, I made a pact with myself:

I would have a different life than Cecelia

To Be Continued......

Summer, 1951

#1 Living in St. Paul

#2 Living in San Francisco

#3 Living in Minneapolis

#4 Moved to Los Angeles to live with Joe W.

#5 Living in Los Angeles with Joe W.

#6, #7 and #8 Lived on the farm until of age.

Trixie lived to be almost 20 years old and died in his sleep in a straw bed in the red barn.

I don't recall FJ ever mentioning Cecelia again.

None of the step children ever went back to the farm to visit FJ. He passed away in 1982.

FJ is buried next to Cecelia in the Catholic Cemetery.

About the Author

#8

Angie is a graduate of Metropolitan State University in St. Paul, MN., with a BA in Writing.

This is her first book of memoirs; a tribute to her mother. She is currently working on an inspirational book about the life of #8, and how it is possible to rise above the past and move on.

She lives in Minnetonka, MN

G mail: olsonangie8

Made in the USA
Middletown, DE
28 September 2024

61190505R00076